AF323086

# *Steubenville*

Winner of the 1992 Pearl Chapbook Contest
Judged by Donna Hilbert

# Julie Herrick White

# Steubenville

*a sequence of poems*

Pearl
Editions

1992

*To Dennis*

The history of Fort Steuben was compiled by the Ohio Historical Society and excerpted from the *Tri-State Trader.*

**Steubenville**
Copyright © 1992 by Julie Herrick White
All rights reserved
Printed in the United States of America

ISBN 0-9628094-3-8

**Pearl Editions**
3030 E. Second Street
Long Beach, California 90803

# Contents

There is a haiku by the poet Bashó which, in R.H. Blyth's translation goes:

> It is deep autumn
> my neighbor,—
> how does he live?

This is a question seldom far from my mind, and in poetry I look for the answer. *Steubenville* is a cycle of poems set in the 1950's in the Italian community of a working class Ohio River town. It chronicles a brief courtship, a brief marriage. Birth and death side by side, in life, in art. All nostalgia evaporates in accurate remembering:

> I was the new girl in the dime store,
> saving money for college.
> We talked about Beethoven
> while we cut windowshades
> in the back of the store.
> I'm from Steubenville, Ohio, he said.
> Do you know where that is?

and:

> I cried every day when I came here,
> the woman said.
>
> The men played pool and played
> hunches on lucky numbers
> while the women said rosaries
> on Wednesday nights, walking home
> together through the heavy air.

A companion question to how does one live, is how does one die? I think of Icarus, of Auden. While we are living our *doggy lives,* who is falling from the sky? In *Steubenville,* it is a regular guy putting on the same wings we each put on every morning to carry us out of bed into work, love, and to more of the same, day after day.

> Fidel Castro is coming to the U.S.,
> he said. Look at his picture.
> I liked his out-law look,
> feeling angry too,
> tired of housework and winter colds.

He didn't notice,
just getting over a gall bladder attack
as he was, having missed two weeks' work
at his new job, looking tired
and worried about life insurance.

In Steubenville is grief the same black powder in the chest as it is at
my desk in Cerritos?

    . . . Her grief was louder than mine.
The family's grief, taken in total,
was the loudest I had ever heard.


What set *Steubenville* apart from several other excellent manu-
scripts, was that with each reading, I remained moved. These are
poems of authentic experience: simple, unsentimental. They are
without verbal or stylistic pyrotechnics to convince us of their impor-
tance. The power is in the story; in the story of our neighbor's life
we glimpse our own. What can be made from ordinary suffering?
Julie Herrick White's answer is *Steubenville,* a work of extraordinary
beauty.

—DONNA HILBERT
October, 1992

*vii*

In the Fifties . . .

*In 1789 a settlement was made on the Indian shore of the Ohio River.  Fort Steuben was named for the Prussian drillmaster of the Continental Army, Baron Frederick William von Steuben.*

*

"Steubenville is a black crust."
—*James Wright*

# The Dime Store

It was Christmas in the dime store,
and I met him there
exchanging jokes with Santa Claus.
A nice guy, he said to me later.
Speaks five languages, including Armenian.

It was Christmas in the dime store
with special nativity calendars
and coffee and celebrating
and spun glass ornaments
hanging from the most perfect branches.

Hell, you don't have to dust,
he said to me.
You can dust after Christmas.
And I watched him
and wondered who he was
and where he got his funny authority
over us
       in three weeks' time.

# *Places of Origin*

They had transferred him
to this cold town in Michigan,
the Italian-immigrant-dime-store-manager.
He had all of Beethoven's symphonies
on record, and the Violin Concerto in D.
He played them nights in his rented room
while Lake Michigan wrecked more pilings
at the bottom of that winter town.

He was a long way from Heiligenstadt,
but he knew the landscape of the third movements
like the inside of his hand.

I was the new girl in the dime store,
saving money for college.
We talked about Beethoven
while we cut window shades
in the back of the store.
I'm from Steubenville, Ohio, he said.
Do you know where that is?


# *Concert*


The local symphony
was playing Beethoven's Fourth,
and we sat together on chilly metal chairs
in the high school gym.

He does not belong here, I thought,
he with the red silk necktie,
and the wind blew gales of snow
around that dismal building.

Afterwards we got stuck
on an untraveled road in the park.
We will make our own road, he said bravely,
having kissed me in a grove of trees
we never found again.

# Directions

To get to Steubenville, you take the Ohio
Turnpike, he said.
> You want me to turn Catholic, I said.  Why is
> Benedetto Croce on the Index?
Don't worry about the Index, he said.  You can
take the Turnpike all the way across Ohio.
It's an easy trip.  I've got a job there now,
a better job.
> How many children do you think we should have?
About four.
> That's too many, I said.
You'll get used to the idea.  You'll like
Italians.  They're so cheerful.
> Cheerful, I said.  Why does the Pope
> have to be infallible?
Cheerful, infallible, what's the difference?
They've got a Catholic college there now,
and their basketball's terrific.
> How many miles? I said.
I don't know, but you get off the Turnpike
at Youngstown.
> I'm not worried about Youngstown, I said.
> I'm worried about how many miles.

*

*The Fort was a log structure, constructed on the second of three natural terraces, some 300 feet from the Ohio River.*

*

> Is that where they make Steuben glass?
> my mother's friend asked.
> > I don't think so, I said.
> What do they make there?
> > I don't know.

# *A Plateful of Ribbons*

All summer they planned for the shower,
his mother and two sisters.
They rented a cafeteria on Sunday
and served fried chicken and coleslaw
and rolls.  Then they played bingo.

My sister was thirteen.  She came with me.

I wrote down
each person's name beside the gift.
They were collecting the ribbons,
fastening them to a paper plate.
The ribbons grew larger and larger,
covering the plate, covering each other.
This will bring you good luck, they said.
I thanked everyone again.
We packed two cars full of gifts
and drove to his parents' house.
There was much excitement and second
unwrappings and counting the money.
His mother, who could not read English,
had to be told in Italian
how much each person gave.

That night in our bedroom
my sister started to cry.
I don't like this place, she said.
I don't want you to live here.

*

# Rosaries and Lucky Numbers

It was Little Europe,
set on the edge of steel mills
and smoking chimneys.

It was Little Europe
with its Old World beds of geraniums
and saints' statues.

The Italian was faithful to his garden,
yet the stone faces darkened over the years
and geranium leaves rusted away.

I cried every day when I came here,
the woman said.

The men played pool and played
hunches on lucky numbers
while the women said rosaries
on Wednesday nights, walking home
together through the heavy air.

## *Bruises on the Soul: the Mother*

In confession she spoke Italian.
She told what the neighbors
said about her.
She told how the grocer had cheated her.
Many sorrows, she said.
Many bruises on the soul.

After Mass she always stayed
for one last prayer.  It was the mother
who lit candles and said the special devotions,
and the other women noticed.

With her extra prayers
she could pull her family through
while they waited outside the church,
shuffling their feet, smoking and talking.


## *Going Back: the Father*

When I get some money,
I'm gonna go back for a visit.
See my sister.  See my old village.
I dunno what it's like now,
so many years after the War.
My sister's got a refrigerator now.
Her son works in a factory.
He's got a motorcycle.
                    My God,
I wouldn't know her son if I saw him
on the street.  What's happened to our old
house? I ask her.  What's happened to our old
church?  My God, what's the use
of going back to see strangers?
I think it hurts to go back,
like all those years
it hurt to stay away.

# The Visit

Are you happy? my mother demanded,
galloping into my blue and white tiled kitchen.
I've been so worried about you.
Are you happy?

She had driven the Turnpike
in the '53 station wagon left over
from my father's business.  I told myself
she was nervous and over-reacting from the long drive.

Of course I was happy, I said.
What bride of three months is not happy?


# Leo

Who is she? Leo Vellucci said, frowning.
She's Vince's new wife,
somebody whispered.  She's all right.
Still he frowned.
Leo ran a numbers game
in his grocery store.

Come on, he said, motioning
that I should pay for my bread
and milk first.
The old men waited,
watching me,
holding on to their money.

# Apostolic Blessing

Someone sent us a special
Apostolic Blessing from the Pope.
It was hand-lettered,
and we framed it
and hung it in the livingroom
which had no furniture yet,
and he read *The New York Times* a lot
and worked at the crossword puzzles
and tore exotic recipes
out of the Sunday paper.
I said I had never made Lebanese
curried lamb, but I would try,
and we listened a lot to Beethoven's
Violin Concerto in D, sometimes
in bed since we had no livingroom chairs,
and even in the bedroom
with the curtains closed,
the strong polluted air seemed to
find us, and he didn't ask me
if I liked it here, and I didn't know yet
if I did.

# The Green Grocer's Daughters

The green grocer had three daughters.
The first one was the most beautiful
and didn't stay in Steubenville.

The second one married and had three children.
She didn't have much strength,
but they'd promised the priest
they'd have one more after her husband
finished night school. They kept
their promise, but the woman's
young heart gave out.
That left the green grocer's grandchildren,
four little boys running wild.

Why don't you marry Julia?
the green grocer said, putting his arm around
the husband.  Julia was the last daughter,
not so beautiful,
but already she loved the children,
ironing their little cotton shirts,
even spanking them.

# The Doctor

He knew all the women
and their ailments.  He spoke
to them in Italian.  He knew about
pessaries and hormones and the flu
and homesickness that lasts for thirty years.

He knew about hemorrhages and blood clots
and childbirth and breeches and tearing
and what priests shouted at you
when you confessed to using birth control.

He had lost his own wife on the delivery table
because the Church said,
If it comes to a choice,
save the unbaptized child.
The mother,
having received the Sacraments,
is in a state of grace already.

# *Mike Fink and the Republicans*

Mike Fink was a keelboat man,
known the length of the Ohio.
He was the loudest bragger,
the fiercest fighter.
He was killed in a fight
over an Indian woman.

Steubenville became known
as a dirty Ohio River town,
gambling and prostitutes
and floods in the spring.

A Republican mayor
tried to shut down the prostitutes,
and the Democrats said,
We told you this would happen.
Old women are getting attacked
at bus stops, on the streets.
You should have kept the prostitutes.

All this trouble—
be careful when you go downtown,
my husband said.
I had a job at the Carnegie Library
head of the children's department.
How could I tell them I was pregnant?

# Wednesday

I hated Wednesdays,
doing the wash
in my mother-in-law's basement.
I hated how she re-heated
the water on a gas stove
and used it again.  I hated
the smell of strong soap
and too much bleach.  Moonshine,
as she called it, and she made
the washing last all day.

I do not want these bleached,
I said, taking out my things.

My son tell me all about you,
she said pleasantly.
He show me pictures.
He say, I want her to come for a visit.
He say, If you like, I take.
If you no like, I no take.

*

You are what—*pregnant?*
my mother said.
O my God, not already!

*

*The story of Fort Steuben began in 1785 when the Continental Congress enacted the Northwest Ordinance which provided for a survey of lands west of the Ohio River.*

# The Father Decorates

My father-in-law
had planted our rose bushes
and cut our grass on Saturdays.
He closed the chimneys
on all the fireplaces, saying
that fireplaces were dirty.
You need an electric log, he said.

Leave him alone, his wife said bitterly
when he put up all the Christmas ornaments
himself, unpacking the homemade
manger and the figurines he had bought,
one by one at the dime store.
Leave him alone, she stormed
when he set up the tree
in front of the closed fireplace
and unpacked the Swiss Guards
someone had brought him from Rome.

*

### Pizzelles

*4 eggs, ²/₃ cup melted butter, 1 cup sugar,
2 teasp. vanilla or anise, 2 ²/₃ cups flour.*

*Spoon into a pre-heated iron.
Bake 1 to 2 minutes each.*

# Home

Home is not the Italian Christmas party
when you are there and not Italian.
The women drank anisette.
The men drank whiskey.
Artichokes glistened in olive oil.
The spaghetti tasted like snakes.

# Maria and Dominic

Maria did all her washing by hand,
not trusting a machine.  Maria
and Dominic lived together in sin
because she had a husband somewhere
in Italy, and the Church said
she was still married.

Maria used to keep a rooming house.
The others left, but Dominic stayed on
for twenty-five years.

Dominic worked in the mill
but he didn't drive a car.
All the Italian men
rode the mill bus.

Dominic had a cough
that lingered all year,
shaking the house at night,
the frame house on Railroad Street,
grown deaf on one side
from the mill whistle.

Signora, which saint
will your child be named for?
he asked me in his beautiful,
baritone voice.

# The Fall

They told me stories of my sister-in-law
who fell in her highchair
when they lived in Italy.

They told of her falling on her face
into red-hot fireplace ashes,
and I thought,

is this the fall of man
in the garden, Adam, obstreperous,
rocking his baby highchair,
tipping himself into pain
and sorrow?

The mother wails and cries for help,
babbling of lost perfection.
The child screams,
her white gown soiled,
coal ashes sticking to her,

skin glazed and burning,
too tender
for the priest to touch.

# *The Fort*

The fort was basically square with block houses
set diagonally at each of the corners.
The inside angles of the block houses
were connected with a line of pickets 150 feet long.

Our house, which his father had built,
was basically square and safe.
We had a Hotpoint stove,
a gift from his parents,
and the livingroom furniture
was on order.

Evenings we sat at the kitchen table.
He read the paper;
I worked on the braided rug
I had started in Michigan.

Fidel Castro is coming to the U.S.,
he said.  Look at his picture.
I liked his out-law look,
feeling angry too,
tired of housework and winter colds.

He didn't notice,
just getting over a gall bladder attack
as he was, having missed two weeks' work
at his new job, looking tired
and worried about life insurance.

*

Where did they go, those wonderful glass
ornaments in the dime store window,
those snowflakes that danced and whirled
to the First Movement
and promised us everything?

# I Enter the Ohio Valley Hospital

Fire and steam were already here
in accelerating amounts.
I was having a baby
on that heavy, polluted day
in August.  There was something
wrong with my husband.
I could see it through shadows
and slitted eyelids.

We've never lost a father yet,
they said to him, as he watched me,
gray-faced and perspiring
from some problem of his own.

It was my day, made holy by saints
and white-gowned attendants.
Labor is progressing well,
they said, nodding their heads,
yet he watched, unsanctified.  There was
something wrong, not included in the early
jokes or dime store talk.  It was
the color of sludge and smoke from chimneys.
I had not been noticing.  I had been
engrossed in layettes and little shoes
and flannel receiving blankets.

I should have been a priest, he said,
watching me in misery.
                          Thanks a lot,
I said.  That really helps me now.

# A Question of Grief

Some kind of unlucky accident
over a previous birthmark,
malignancy entered from another
life, perhaps.  Embarrassing,
those other lives, like affairs out of
the past with exotic women.

He should have mentioned it to me,
the birthmark, the other life.

But there was always so much to say,
with arguing about Harry Truman
and the Pendergast machine, with the
New York Yankees always winning.
I hope our first child is a girl,
he had said.  That's why I bought this pink shirt.

The doctor was explaining that the liver
was the secondary site.  After that,
he said, it spreads quickly.

The doctor was explaining this to me
over the sounds of my mother-in-law's
wailing.  Her grief was louder than mine.
The family's grief, taken in total,
was the loudest I had ever heard.

My name is Bonaventure Salvadore,
he said.  But my friends
call me Cal.


*


# *Making Connections*


In a combination of joy and heavy-handed
piety, his mother had named him Bonaventure.
In the little Italian village
they called him *Ventu,* and later
in the dime store in Elyria, Ohio,
his friends, puzzled,
called him *Vince,* as if his name was Vincent.

I realize that his mother
had picked an important saint
who had connections with people like
St. Francis of Assisi and the holy kings
and St. Thomas Aquinas.  Still it was heavy
baggage to carry, and although
his mother screamed out
for all the saints at the end,
none of them
prevented him from dying of cancer
at thirty-five, the same age at which
lucky old Bonaventure
had been chosen General of the Franciscans.

# Questions

My cousin Mary is in limbo;
let us pray.

My forever lost nephew is in limbo;
let us kneel.
Let us toll the bell.

*

Where will you go?
Where will I go?
What is the way out
of limbo but by passing through
tunnels of empty nights
and repeating the story
of a fragile marriage
that gave way
in a few weeks?

You died leaving me
some religious books,
a box of photographs
whose names I do not know,
and the blueprint of a woman
labeled like the parts
of an airplane.

What shall I do with it?

# What We Wore

To lie there in your overdone casket
in the brown suit we hadn't paid for
yet, and to look so serene!
How little I knew about you
except who your mother's family was
and what your politics were
and whether your sister liked
the neighbors and why we didn't buy
the antique rope bed
that I wanted so much.

The kitchen was always a mess,
and the gas tank was always
on empty while you smiled
at me, coasting downhill like an expert,
and the escape
I dreamed of sometimes
was closer than I knew.

How guilty our dreams make us
when they come true in some
treacherous way.  I didn't wear
black.  I wore the blue dress
you loved and insisted was the color
of the sky over Rome—
you who had never seen Rome!

# *We Take the Baby to the Doctor*

It was the same Italian doctor.

My mother-in-law came along.
To help with the baby, she said.
My mother-in-law was an apparition
in black dress and sweater.
Her skin had turned the color
of laundry soap.

He was my son, she said over and over.
Let me die too.

She carried the baby
as we crossed Fourth Street.
I haven't mentioned yet,
it was a girl
and, I thought,
a pretty good one.

She carried the baby over her shoulder:
black against pink, and something
about the combination
I didn't like.

She stepped in front of a truck,
black against pink, laundry soap
against pearl.  I screamed
for the three of us.  I dragged them back.
The truck went by.  I kept on
screaming.  Black dresses and brides
gone wrong— I screamed for all
the slippery edges of love, and life
whistling through the teeth of death
and spots on the funeral home carpet
and a dead man's feet
buried under flowers.

It was finally time to scream
outside
in the middle of the street.
It felt so good.
He should have heard me
and I guess he did.

You can't do that, I said
and took the baby back.

# *Trying on Coats*

Mondays
we wash the gowns of dead saints,
my daughter and I.

Wednesdays
we sweep the sympathy cards under the bed.
Sundays
we try our fur-trimmed church coats,
but they are too heavy for our shoulders,
                                    and I think,
you and your magic dime store,
you and your lucky numbers.
Someone else will play your records now
                                    and rent
your upstairs room; Lake Michigan
makes fresh waterlines every spring.
The maps are too clean,
and the eye sees all the wrong things.

You and Beethoven will not meet each other
except on the inside of your head
                                    or your hands.


*


I suppose
my daughter and I
will cut paper stars
for the next Christmas tree,
not trusting glass,
not knowing whether
to believe in Santa Claus
if he speaks Armenian
                        or Croatian
                        or Serbian
                        or some provincial dialect,
and we will catch ourselves
watching for overseas mail,
not knowing which lost language
brings a message from you.

## *September 30, 1959*

I  I don't blame you for leaving,
    he said to me when it was all over
    and we were back in the kitchen
    watching the movers.  I'd go with you
    if I could, he said over black coffee,
    and I looked at him and looked at him
    but didn't dare answer.


II  I took the Turnpike
    with my daughter,
    heading west
    in a used Dodge Lancer.

    It was not my car,
    still his,
    yet they said
    I owned the title.


III  The site of Fort Steuben is just
    north of Adams Street along the west
    side of SR7.  All that remains
    today are four stone posts.

JULIE HERRICK WHITE has published a chapbook of poems, *Friends from the Other Side,* and a collection of short stories, *Uncle Gust and the Temple of Healing.* In 1992, she received an Individual Artist Fellowship from the Indiana Arts Commission. White lives in South Bend, Indiana, with her husband. She has one daughter.